TANKS AT WAR

Lynn Leslie Peppas

CRABTREE
Publishing Company
www.crabtreebooks.com

Crabtree Publishing Company
www.crabtreebooks.com

Dedicated by Lynn Leslie Peppas
To my son, Nicholas, a big fan of all things tank

Author: Lynn Leslie Peppas
**Publishing plan research
and development**: Reagan Miller
Project coordinator: Crystal Sikkens
Editors: Sonya Newland, Crystal Sikkens
Proofreader: Janine Deschenes
Designer: Tim Mayer
Map: Stefan Chabluk
Cover design: Ken Wright
**Production coordinator and
prepress technician**: Ken Wright
Print coordinator: Margaret Amy Salter
Production coordinated by: White-Thomson
Publishing

Photographs:
Alamy: Everett Collection: pp. 18–19; Chronicle:
pp. 20-21; RIA Novosti: pp. 26–27; p. 40: Stocktrek
Images, Inc.: p. 40; Agencja Fotograficzna Caro: p.
44; Bridgeman Art Library: Tanks, Somme (w/c),
Handley-Read, Captain Edward Henry (1869-
1935) / Topham Picture Source, Edenbridge,
Kent, UK: p. 17; Corbis: Berliner Verlag: pp.
28–29; Bettmann: p. 30; Henri Bureau/Sygma:
pp. 32–33; Christopher Morris/VII: p. 36; Sergei
Chirikov/epa: pp. 38–39; iStock: Rockfinder: p.
12; Shutterstock: cover; Rocksweeper: pp. 1, 6-7;
Trybex: p. 7; Gary Blakeley: p. 8; BlueRingMedia:
pp. 8–9; Sergey Kamshylin: pp. 10, 24;
PhotoStock10: pp. 12–13; Everett Historical: pp.
14–15; mcseem: pp. 22–23; Mikael Damkier: p. 25;
Opachevsky Irina: p. 33; U.S. Air Force: Roland
Balik: p. 42; U.S. Department of Defense Images:
pp. 3, 11, 34–35, 43; Wikimedia: p. 16; U.S. Navy:
p. 5; Skyring: p. 21; Lieutenant General John H.
Hay, Jr./U.S. Army: p. 31; Shane A. Cuomo, U.S.
Air Force: p. 37; John J. Pistone/U.S. Army: p. 41;
Simta: p. 45.

Library and Archives Canada Cataloguing in Publication

Peppas, Lynn, author
    Tanks at war / Lynn Peppas.

(Crabtree chrome)
Includes index.
Issued in print and electronic formats.
ISBN 978-0-7787-2294-6 (bound).--ISBN 978-0-7787-2233-5
(paperback).--ISBN 978-1-4271-8089-6 (html)

    1. Tanks (Military science)--Juvenile literature. I. Title.
II. Series: Crabtree chrome

UG446.5.P466 2016   j623.7'4752   C2015-907959-4
                                            C2015-907960-8

Library of Congress Cataloging-in-Publication Data

Names: Peppas, Lynn, author.
Title: Tanks at war / Lynn Peppas.
Description: New York : Crabtree Publishing Company,
[2016] | Series: Crabtree chrome | Includes index. |
Description based on print version record and CIP data
provided by publisher; resource not viewed.
Identifiers: LCCN 2015045729 (print) | LCCN 2015045142
(ebook) | ISBN 9781427180896 (electronic HTML) | ISBN
9780778722946 (reinforced library binding : alk. paper) |
ISBN 9780778722335 (pbk. : alk. paper)
Subjects: LCSH: Tanks (Military science)--History.
Classification: LCC UG446.5 (print) | LCC UG446.5 .P363
2016 (ebook) | DDC
 358.1/883--dc23
LC record available at http://lccn.loc.gov/2015045729

Crabtree Publishing Company
www.crabtreebooks.com   1-800-387-7650

Printed in Canada/022016/MA20151130

Published in Canada
Crabtree Publishing
616 Welland Ave.
St. Catharines, ON
L2M 5V6

Published in the United States
Crabtree Publishing
PMB 59051
350 Fifth Avenue, 59th Floor
New York, New York 10118

Published in the United Kingdom
Crabtree Publishing
Maritime House
Basin Road North, Hove
BN41 1WR

Published in Australia
Crabtree Publishing
3 Charles Street
Coburg North
VIC 3058

Contents

Beasts of the Battlefield

Operation Desert Storm

February 1991. U.S. troops had been traveling in tanks for days through the Iraqi desert. Outside, the rain poured violently. The passing sandstorms were blinding, and the tank drivers had no roads to follow. Instead, they found their way using **GPS** (Ground Positioning System). No one had ever used this before.

> **Tanks have been used in warfare for about 100 years. The first tank was used on September 15, 1916.**

◀ *This map shows where the Battle of 73 Easting took place.*

The Battle of 73 Easting

On February 26, U.S. tanks finally arrived at a place in the desert known as 73 Easting. There, they braced themselves for battle against the Iraqi army, known as the Iraqi Republican Guard (IRG). The soldiers could hardly see because of a sandstorm. Thermal sights—devices that locate objects by the heat they give off—helped them find the enemy tanks. With the help of these new technologies, the U.S. only lost one tank at the end of the fierce battle.

▲ *The Iraqi Republican Guard lost about 100 tanks during the Battle of 73 Easting.*

GPS: a system that uses signals from satellites to determine locations

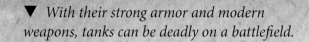
▼ *With their strong armor and modern weapons, tanks can be deadly on a battlefield.*

Battle-Ready Tanks

Tanks, or Armored Combat Vehicles (ACVs), are fighting vehicles protected by heavy armor. They can drive easily through the most difficult landscapes. Even terrible weather cannot stop them. Modern tanks have technology that helps soldiers find their way, or locate their enemies in fog or sandstorms.

Technology Race

Designing and building tanks with the best technology is a never-ending race. A country may make armor that will protect a tank from the deadliest **artillery**. But it is never long before another country develops weapons and ammunition, such as bullets and shells, that can damage that armor.

The Italian artist and inventor, Leonardo da Vinci, drew a plan for a battle tank in 1487. This was more than 400 years before the first tank was ever driven!

▲ *This is a model of the tank that Leonardo da Vinci designed. It was made of wood covered in metal plates.*

artillery: large weapons that can shoot long distances

Armored Fighting Vehicles

Tanks are built to carry out different jobs on the battlefield. The first tanks were grouped as heavy, medium, or light. The group they were in depended on their weight, gun size, amount of armor, and their purpose in battle. Later, heavy and medium tanks became known as Main Battle Tanks (MBTs).

main battle gun: mounted on the turret; shoots the heaviest ammunition

hull: the body of a tank that holds the engine, computer, crew members, and tracks

▼ *Heavy tanks are the biggest armored fighting vehicles, with the most powerful guns and ammunition.*

Light Tanks

Light tanks include armored cars and fighting vehicles used by soldiers fighting on foot. Most light tanks have guns or cannons, but their main roles are to **scout** out dangerous areas or to carry large numbers of soldiers.

turret: a round armored weapon platform that holds the main gun or cannon and/or machine guns. It sits on top of a tank and rotates in a full circle.

caterpillar tracks: metal linked treads turned by wheels

Explosive Reactive Armor (ERA) is a special type of tank armor. It is made of linked metal boxes, filled with explosives. When hit by heavy ammunition, ERA explodes outward to protect the tank.

scout: to search an area for information

A Tank's Worst Enemies

Anti-tank guns are large guns or cannons that shoot ammunition that can stop a tank in its tracks. Some anti-tank guns are towed to the battlefield, while others are self-propelled, or able to move using their own engine. There are some anti-tank guns that look like tanks, but they do not have the same strong armor. Howitzers are anti-tank guns with short gun barrels.

◀ *Anti-tank mines are weapons that are planted in the ground. They explode when the weight of a tank rolls over them.*

During World War II, the German army made tank traps by widening the deep ditches in the ground known as trenches. A trench that was the same size as—or longer than—a tank's tracks could stop it dead.

Armor-Piercing Ammunition

High-explosive anti-tank (HEAT) shells contain explosives with a copper lining in the tip of the bullet. Upon contact, the copper melts and the explosive pushes the shell through the tank's armor. SABOT is a narrow metal dart or arrow that sits inside a shell. The shell fills the large **barrel** of a gun but falls away from the dart after it is shot. HEAT and SABOT can both injure or kill tank crews.

▲ *The tip of a SABOT dart is smaller than a quarter.*
SABOTs can travel at 3,500 mph (5,600 km/h).

barrel: the long "nose" of a gun

Tank Crews

In a battle situation, most MBTs need at least four people to operate them. While **deployed**, crews may have to live inside their tank for days. The driver sits in a tiny, tight space at the front. He or she has to lean far back in the chair to fit. The commander works in the turret. Commanders communicate with other tanks and tell the crew what to do.

◀ *It is very cramped inside a tank—there are no beds or showers.*

▶ *The gunner uses "sights" to target the enemy. These devices have night-vision so they can be used in the dark as well as daylight.*

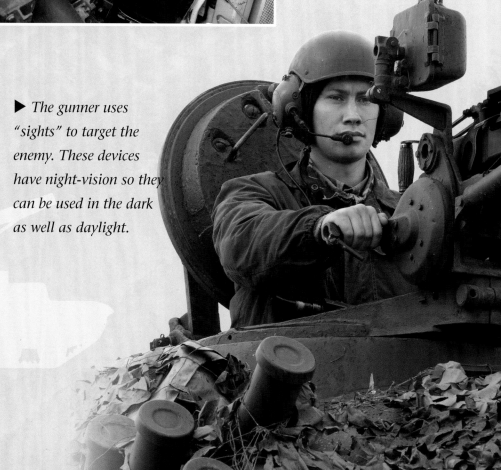

The Gunner's Role

The gunner is in charge of firing the turret gun as well as the main battle gun. Laser range-finders help a gunner by using a laser beam to measure the distance to a target. Once the gunner pinpoints the target, he or she tells the loader what ammunition to put into the main gun.

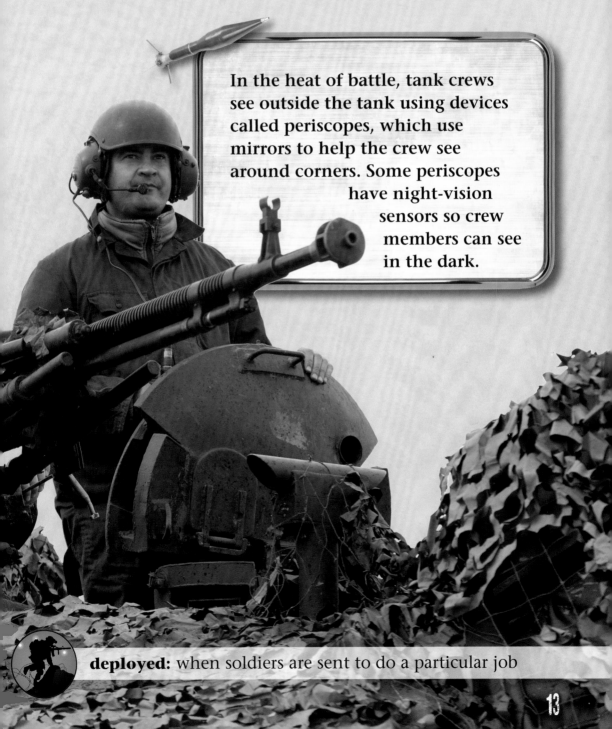

In the heat of battle, tank crews see outside the tank using devices called periscopes, which use mirrors to help the crew see around corners. Some periscopes have night-vision sensors so crew members can see in the dark.

deployed: when soldiers are sent to do a particular job

Tanks in World War I

Trench Warfare

During World War I, soldiers shot at their enemy from inside trenches. Barbed wire was placed in front of trenches to stop attacking soldiers from reaching them. Trench warfare resulted in long battles where many men were killed, but where no side gained land or victories.

The British called their Armored Fighting Vehicle a "water tank." This name threw off the enemy. They believed it was a tank used to hold water. The name "tank" stuck and is still used today.

Mother of All Tanks

The British wanted to break the **stalemate**. Their navy began designing and building an armed and armored vehicle that would help British soldiers attack enemy trenches. In 1916, they revealed the result—a type of "land ship" that ran on tracks. One hundred of these tanks were built. They became known as the Mark I.

▼ *Britain's new secret weapon had to drive through mud and over rocks and large potholes while protecting soldiers. The earliest designs were armed with large guns and machine guns that shot bullets continuously.*

stalemate: an outcome with no winner

The Battle of the Somme

In 1916, the **Allies** launched an attack at the Somme, France, where their German enemies had created a strong system of trenches. The Battle of the Somme lasted many months. Thousands of Allied soldiers died every day. Still they could not defeat the Germans. The British decided to unleash their secret weapon.

"We heard strange throbbing noises, and lumbering slowly toward us came three huge mechanical monsters...Big metal things they were, with two sets of caterpillar wheels that went right round the body."

Bert Chaney, British Signal Officer

▼ *During World War I, tanks were known as male or female. Male tanks (like this one) fought with two large guns and three machine guns. Female tanks had five machine guns.*

▲ *Forty-nine Mark I tanks were brought to the Somme,*
but many broke down before they could be used in battle.

Mechanical Monsters

On September 15, 1916, 15 British tanks went
roaring onto the battlefield for the first time. No one
had seen anything like the tanks before. German
soldiers panicked at the sight of them. But despite
their new weapon, the Allies gained only 1 mile
(1.6 kilometers) of land. Many tanks were caught in
ditches, broke down, or were stopped by artillery fire.

Allies: countries such as Britain, France, Russia, and Canada

The Battle of Cambrai

The Germans also held a strong trench system in another part of France, called Cambrai. The Allies planned to use tanks to defeat the enemy here, but they were worried that the tanks would not be able to cross the trenches. To solve this problem, some tanks carried bundles of wood to drop in the trenches. This would help the tanks cross over into battle.

▼ *The tanks used in the Battle of Cambrai were Mark IVs, which had much stronger armor than earlier versions.*

Success at Last!

More than 400 tanks were secretly brought to Cambrai. Early in the morning of November 20, 1917, soldiers began laying out the bridges. The plan worked perfectly. With the help of tanks, the Allies **advanced** about 5 miles (8 kilometers) and captured around 8,000 German soldiers.

"The barbed wire neither stopped our tank nor broke up and wound round the tracks as we had feared, but squashed flat as we moved forward and remained flat."

A tank crew member describing the Battle of Cambrai

advanced: moved forward

The Battle of Amiens

The Battle of Amiens was the largest tank battle of World War I. The Allies secretly brought in more than 600 tanks before the battle began. Some of these were the new British Mark V tanks. They had more powerful engines and better tracks. The hull was designed with slits so the crew could see better. Another gun was added to the rear.

▼ *Before Amiens, Germany had been winning the war. That changed when the British tanks rolled onto the battlefield.*

The only tanks that Germany made during World War I were about 20 A7V tanks. The first German tank was used in battle in March 1918. It carried one main gun and six machine guns.

Black Day of the German Army

The surprise attack at Amiens began on August 8, 1918. Tanks led the way and protected the **infantry** soldiers following behind. Tanks shot and killed enemy machine-gunners. More than 20,000 German soldiers died. The Germans called the first day of the Battle of Amiens "Black Day." This defeat was the turning point in the war.

▲ *The German A7V tanks could each hold up to 18 soldiers.*

infantry: soldiers on foot

Tanks in World War II

Blitzkrieg!

Tanks became even more important in battlefield victories in World War II. This war began in September 1939, when the German leader Adolf Hitler ordered the invasion of Poland. The Germans used the combined **tactics** of speed and surprise in their invasion. This became known as "Blitzkrieg," which means "lightning war."

"Today we are crushed by the sheer weight of the mechanized forces hurled against us, but we can still look to a future in which even greater mechanized force will bring us victory."

French General Charles de Gaulle, after the Germans invaded France

German Tanks Take Action

German armored tank units—called Panzer divisions—played a new role in warfare. The Panzer MBTs quickly broke through weak enemy lines, with support from artillery and attacks from aircraft. The Germans used Blitzkrieg successfully against other European countries in the first few years of World War II.

▼ *German tank divisions rushed in and created chaos behind enemy lines.*

tactics: the way that a battle is carried out

Tank Race

The Allies produced thousands more tanks than the
Axis Powers in World War II. These included 84,000
Russian-made T-34s. At the beginning of World War II,
the T-34 was the best tank on the battlefield. In 1942,
Germany created two new types of tanks, called Tiger
and Panther, which were a deadly threat to the Allies.
However, Germany could not build enough of them.

▲ *The T-34 design remained in*
service for over 20 years—longer
than any other tank.

▲ *The Allied tanks at El Alamein included the mighty American Sherman tanks.*

El Alamein

Germany's Panzer divisions were winning the battles in North Africa, but they were running low on fuel and ammunition. The Allies used this to their advantage. During the Second Battle of El Alamein in Egypt, they used more than 800 tanks against the Germans. The Germans had around 400 tanks, but within a few weeks only 20 were left fighting. The Germans were soon forced to retreat.

At the Second Battle of El Alamein, Allied tanks had to cross a dangerous 5-mile (8-kilometer) wide anti-tank minefield called the "Devil's Garden" to reach the enemy.

Axis Powers: the combined forces of Germany, Italy, and Japan

The Battle of Kursk

The biggest tank battle of World War II was the Battle of Kursk. By 1943, the Russian, then called Soviet, army had formed a strong line of defense around the Russian city of Kursk. On July 4, Germany attacked Kursk with thousands of tanks at both ends of the line. But the Soviets had many more tanks—they were ready to fight back!

Amphibious tanks were first used for warfare during World War II. Some were used during the D-Day landings in 1944, when Allied forces launched a surprise attack on the Germans at Normandy, France, after crossing the English Channel.

Prokhorovka

As the German tanks began gaining ground toward Kursk, the Russian Fifth Guards Tank Army set out to face them. The two sides met near the Russian city of Prokhorovka. The Soviets started with more tanks, but they also lost more than the Germans in the battle. Despite this, on August 23, the German army finally gave up and retreated. The Allies had won.

▼ *During the Battle of Kursk, the Soviet army destroyed hundreds of German Panther and Tiger tanks.*

amphibious: made to work on or in water

German Tank Aces

A tank ace is a hero who "kills" or destroys the most tanks during a war. German tank ace Kurt Knispel was a loader, gunner, and tank commander. He is World War II's **ace of aces** with 168 Allied tank kills. Tank commander Michael Wittman is another famous German tank ace. On one occasion, he destroyed 14 Allied tanks in 15 minutes.

"Wittman was a Nazi [German] from the start. It didn't matter who killed him, just that he was killed."

British tank gunner, Joe Ekins, reported to have killed Michael Wittman in battle in 1944

Allied Aces

Soviet tank commander, Dmitry Lavrinenko, was the Allied tank ace of aces in World War II. He had over 50 tank kills in his T-34. Canadian tank ace, Sydney Valpy Radley-Walters—known as "Captain Rad"—figured out that there was a weak spot at the base of the turret on the German Tiger tank. This information helped other Allied tank crews destroy German tanks.

▼ *Soldiers on both sides would compete with each other to get the most enemy tank "kills."*

ace of aces: the best ace within a group

Tanks in Modern Conflicts

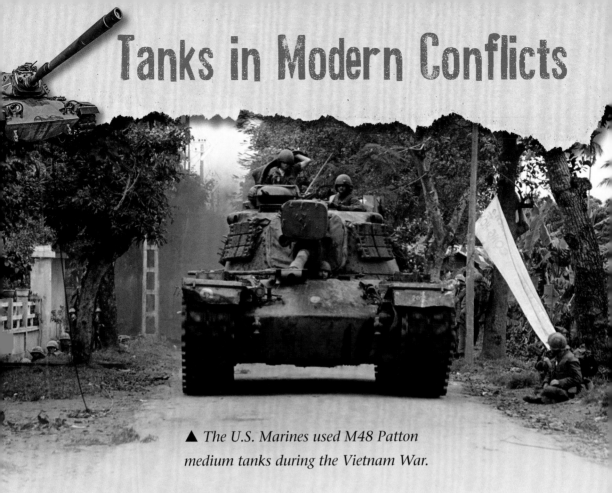

▲ *The U.S. Marines used M48 Patton medium tanks during the Vietnam War.*

The Vietnam War

Between 1954 and 1975, North and South Vietnam were at war. The USA joined forces with South Vietnam. U.S. troops used the newly designed M48 Patton tanks as MBTs. The turret and hull had stronger, cast steel armor. The turret was curved, which gave better protection. The M48 came with a larger gun.

"The heavy sniper fire was coming from the church steeple on the left... The tank commander aimed the tank cannon at the steeple. Then there was a thunderous boom and the steeple came tumbling down onto the street."

James M. Mueller, Jr., a soldier in the Vietnam War

Battle for Hue

On January 31, 1968, North Vietnam invaded the city of Hue, South Vietnam. This began the longest and bloodiest battle of the Vietnam War. Once inside the city walls, **snipers** and machine-gunners hid in buildings and began firing on the South Vietnamese. U.S. armored tanks, including the M113 Armored Personnel Carriers (APC), were used to help drive the North Vietnamese back.

▲ *The M113 APCs were amphibious, so they were very useful in the swamps and rivers of Vietnam.*

snipers: skilled shooters who work from a hidden position

▶ *Israel used British-made Centurion tanks during the Yom Kippur War.*

The Yom Kippur War

In October 1973, a **coalition** that included Egypt and Syria launched a surprise attack on Israel during the religious holiday of Yom Kippur. They hoped to force Israel to leave the areas of Sinai and Golan Heights in the Middle East. The coalition had many more tanks, artillery, and soldiers than the Israeli army.

After the Yom Kippur War, the Israelis named the valley at Golan Heights the "Valley of Tears" because of all the soldiers who died in the battle there.

The Battle for the Valley of Tears

At Golan Heights, less than 200 Israeli Centurion tanks positioned on top of a hill were outnumbered by about 1,000 Syrian T-62 tanks in the valley below. The battle went on until only seven Israeli tanks remained. Thirteen damaged Israeli tanks operated by injured Israeli soldiers came to their rescue. They helped Israel win the battle.

◀ *A Syrian T-55 and Israeli Centurion tank stand as a memorial to the battle in the Valley of Tears.*

coalition: a group of countries that join military forces

The Gulf War

In August 1990, Iraqi leader, Saddam Hussein, ordered his army to invade Kuwait. Thousands of Iraqi tanks **spearheaded** the invasion, including Soviet-made tanks such as the T-72. The USA, Britain, and 27 other countries formed a coalition to stop Iraq. This marked the start of the First Gulf War.

"The turrets were flipping 40 ... 50 feet in the air. [...] It was incredible to see a gun tube and the turret just spinning up in the air and landing hundreds of yards away from the (tanks)."

U.S. Sergeant John Scaglione, describing an Iraqi tank being destroyed

Operation Desert Storm

Over 1,800 American M1A1 MBTs joined the coalition fight in the Iraqi desert known as Operation Desert Storm. Their large guns were able to shoot distances of over 1.5 miles (2.5 kilometers). This was about half a mile farther than the Iraqi tank guns could shoot. These powerful tanks helped the USA and its allies defeat Iraqi forces in 100 hours.

▲ *The M1A1 Abrams tank had serious firepower and could travel at up to 42 mph (68 km/h).*

spearheaded: led an attack

Second Gulf War

In March 2003, a coalition of counties including the USA and Britain went to war with Iraq again. This time they hoped to rid the country of Saddam Hussein's government. The USA believed the Iraqis had nuclear bombs, which made them a dangerous enemy. The **campaign**—known as Operation Iraqi Freedom—began with air bombings. These were quickly followed by a ground invasion spearheaded by tanks.

▲ *A U.S.-led coalition invaded Iraq in 2003.*

▲ *Bradley Fighting Vehicles are special armored vehicles used for transporting infantry soldiers during battle.*

Battle for Baghdad

In April, coalition forces invaded Iraq's capital city, Baghdad. The armored attack on Baghdad, called Operation Thunder Run, included M1A1 Abrams and Bradley Fighting Vehicles. Heat exhaustion was a big risk for crews inside these vehicles. Temperatures in the tanks reached more than 100° Fahrenheit (38° Celsius).

Tactical internet is a secure communications system that cannot be jammed by the enemy. In the Gulf War, it allowed coalition forces to talk to one another safely.

campaign: a series of battles planned to achieve victory in war

The South Ossetia War

The state of South Ossetia declared its independence from the country of Georgia in August 2008. This sparked a five-day battle between them. Georgian tanks, including T-72 MBTs, attacked the city of Tskhinvali in South Ossetia. Russia set up a military **compound** there to help the South Ossetians.

The Battle of Tskhinvali

There was fierce fighting between the Georgian and Russian tanks. Three Russian BMP-1s were destroyed, killing all their crew members. The Russians fired back with a rocket-propelled grenade. This is a powerful form of ammunition launched by a rocket. It destroyed one of the T-72s. The conflict ended a few days later, when the Georgian army withdrew.

◀ *Russia sent tanks and armored personnel carriers to support the South Ossetians in their battle with Georgia.*

BMP-1s are amphibious infantry fighting vehicles. They carry eight passengers plus a three-person crew. They can travel at up to 40 mph (60 km/h) on roads and about 5 mph (8 km/h) in water.

compound: a protected area that contains buildings and barracks

The Future of Tanks

Changing Roles for Tanks

Today, soldiers are often sent to countries for peacekeeping duties. Tanks with caterpillar tracks are heavy, expensive to transport, and travel slowly. They can ruin roads. Seeing tanks rolling through their towns and villages can scare **civilians**. For all these reasons, wheeled armored vehicles are used more often than tanks in peacekeeping missions.

▼ *LAV IIIs are wheeled armored vehicles that have run-flat tires. These are special tires that can travel for miles even if they have been punctured.*

▲ *The main gun on a Stryker is either a large machine gun or a*
grenade launcher.

LAV III/STRYKER

Light Armored Vehicles (LAV) such as the Stryker (U.S.) or
LAV III (Canada) are armored vehicles with six, eight, or 12
wheels. They send power to each wheel separately, which
helps them drive over almost any surface. They can travel
at speeds of up to 60 mph (100 km/h).

Shockwaves are violent forces of energy from
explosions. They often cause the most damage to
tanks. A shockwave passing through a tank can
harm the structure, systems, and crew inside.

civilians: people who do not belong to the armed forces

Future Fights

Modern conflicts are global and often arise quickly. Countries need to be able to **mobilize** a combat force at any time, and place it around the world within four days. Armored vehicles, such as tanks, may need to be transported to a battleground by air. The great weight of tanks makes this difficult.

▲ *Huge aircraft are needed to transport tanks to battlegrounds around the world.*

▶ *Some MBTs, such as the U.S. M1A2 Abrams, weigh over 62 tons (56 metric tons)!*

MBTs Still Rule

In 2009, the U.S. Army canceled its Future Combat Systems (FCS) program. This had planned to design lighter armored vehicles so the army could mobilize easier and faster. U.S. military leaders scrapped the project because they felt their troops needed the heavy-armor protection of MBTs.

Today's modern conflicts may be fought with smaller rebel groups that fight against a government. These groups often use weapons such as roadside bombs and rocket-propelled guns. Soldiers need the heavy armor of MBTs to protect them in battle.

mobilize: to get an army ready for war

Future Tank-nology

Tanks are expensive to build—one M1A1 Abrams tank costs over $4 million! For this reason, most countries **upgrade** their tanks with new technologies instead of replacing them. Engineers create better technologies to make MBTs faster, safer, and deadlier to the enemy.

▲ *New technology allows tank commanders to know exactly where their allies—and their enemies—are on the battlefield.*

AdaptIV is the latest technology to hide a tank from its enemies. It can change the temperature of a tank to confuse enemy heat-seeking missiles.

▲ *The South Korean K2 Black Panther is one of the most advanced tanks in the world today.*

Think-Tanks

Smart Armor is tank armor that has special built-in sensors that figure out what kind of ammunition it is being hit with. It also knows how much damage has been done to the tank. Many tanks also now have computer systems with Wireless Tactical Internet. This works with GPS and can share information with up to 1,000 military computers.

upgrade: replace with something better

Learning More

Books

Tank Warfare
by Antony Loveless
(Crabtree, 2009)

Tanks
by Allan Morey
(Bullfrog Books, 2015)

Land Warfare
by Martin J. Dougherty
(Gareth Stevens Publishing,
2010)

Websites

www.tankmuseum.org
The Tank Museum website, with photographs, war stories, virtual tank museum, and more.

www.tanks-encyclopedia.com
Lists tanks by wars and countries.

www.tanks.net
Tanks used in wars throughout history, including anti-tank weapons, tank battles, and tank crews.

http://armedforcesmuseum. com/five-top-tank- commanders-of-world-war-ii/
Top five tank commanders of World War II.

Glossary

ace of aces The best ace within a group

advanced Moved forward

Allies: Countries such as Britain, France, Russia, and Canada, that joined together to fight against the Axis Powers

amphibious Made to work on or in water

artillery Large weapons that can shoot long distances

Axis Powers The combined forces of Germany, Italy, and Japan

barrel The long "nose" of a gun

campaign A series of battles planned to achieve victory in war

civilians People who do not belong to the armed forces

coalition A group of countries that join military forces

compound A protected area that contains buildings and barracks

deployed When soldiers are sent to do a particular job

GPS (Ground Positioning System) A system that uses signals from satellites in space to determine locations

infantry Soldiers on foot

mobilize To get an army ready for war

scout To search an area for information

snipers Skilled shooters who work from a hidden position

spearheaded Led an attack

stalemate An outcome with no winner

tactics The way that a battle is carried out

upgrade Replace with something better

Index

Entries in **bold** refer to pictures